PETS' GUIDES

Kitty's Guide to

Caring for Your Cat

Anita Ganeri

Heinemann
LIBRARY
Chicago, Illinois

Edited by Daniel Nunn, Rebecca Rissman, and Sian Smith
Designed by Cynthia Della-Rovere
Original illustrations © Capstone Global Library Ltd 2013
Illustrated by Rick Peterson
Picture research by Tracy Cummins
Production by Victoria Fitzgerald
Originated by Capstone Global Library Ltd
Printed in China

17 16 15 14 13 12
10 9 8 7 6 5 4 3 2 1

Library of Congress Cataloging-in-Publication Data
Ganeri, Anita, 1961-
Kitty's guide to caring for your cat / Anita Ganeri.—1st ed.
    p. cm.—(Pets' guides)
Includes bibliographical references and index.
ISBN 978-1-4329-7130-4 (hb)—ISBN 978-1-4329-7137-3 (pb) 1. Cats—Juvenile literature. I. Title.
SF447.G246 2013
636.8—dc23   2012017277

Acknowledgments
The author and publisher are grateful to the following for permission to reproduce copyright material: Alamy p. 27 (© Catchlight Visual Services); Capstone Library pp. 11, 15, 23 (Karon Dubke); Getty Images pp. 7 (Antonio Perez/Chicago Tribune/MCT), 9 (Thomas Northcut), 17 (Steve Lyne); iStockphoto pp. 5 (© Louis-Paul St-Onge), 19 (© Michelle Gibson); Shutterstock pp. 13 bottom (© photomak), 13 top (© martellostudio),21 (© Alin Popescu), 25 (© Monkey Business Images).

Cover photograph of a kitten reproduced with permission of Getty Images (Lasse Pattersson). Design elements reproduced with permission of Shutterstock (© Picsfive) and Shutterstock (© R-studio).

We would like to thank Gemma Lovegrove, Veterinary Manager at Cats Protection, for her invaluable help in the preparation of this book.

Every effort has been made to contact copyright holders of any material reproduced in this book. Any omissions will be rectified in subsequent printings if notice is given to the publisher.

All the Internet addresses (URLs) given in this book were valid at the time of going to press. However, due to the dynamic nature of the Internet, some addresses may have changed, or sites may have changed or ceased to exist since publication. While the author and publisher regret any inconvenience this may cause readers, no responsibility for any such changes can be accepted by either the author or the publisher.

Contents

Some words are shown in bold, **like this**. You can find out what they mean by looking in the glossary.

Do You Want a Pet Cat?

Hi! I'm Kitty the cat, and this book is all about cats like me! Did you know that there are millions of pet cats like me? Cats are fun and friendly, but you need to look after us properly for the whole of our lives.

Being a good pet owner means making sure that I always have food, water, and a safe, clean place to live. Then I'll quickly become your best friend.

Choosing Your Cat

Cats can be different colors and sizes. They can have long hair or short hair, like mine. The best place to find your pet cat is at an animal shelter. They have many cats and kittens that need good homes.

Do you want a cat or a kitten? Kittens look cute, but they need lots of special care and attention. You need to spend plenty of time playing with them. You might want to get an adult cat like me instead.

A Healthy Cat

Choose a cat like me with a clean, shiny coat and clear, bright eyes. It should also have clean ears and a dry, clean bottom. A cat that has a runny nose may not be well.

Some cats are very playful and friendly.
Others are shy. Pick a cat that fits in with your
family. A shy cat might find it difficult to be in
a family with very small children.

Getting Ready

It's almost time to bring me home, but there are a few things for you to get ready first. Here is my cat-tastic cat shopping list…

Kitty's Shopping List

- a cat bed or basket
- **litter box** and **cat litter**
- a **scratching post**
- a food bowl
- a water bowl
- cat food
- a brush for **grooming**
- cat toys

Welcome Home

The day has come for me to go to my new home. You can carry me in a special plastic basket. Line it with newspaper and a cozy blanket or towel. You can use the basket later when you take me to visit the vet.

At home, put my bed in a quiet, warm place where I can sleep without being disturbed. If you have other pets, introduce me to them slowly. Keep me indoors for the first three to four weeks. I'll need to go to the bathroom in my **litter box**.

Pick Me Up

Cats like me love to be stroked, especially on our ears and chests. If I rub my head against your hand, that's my way of telling you that I'm happy. Purrrr! But if my tail starts to twitch, it means that I'm getting fed up.

You can pick me up, but please do it gently and use both hands. Put one hand around my bottom and back legs to support my weight. If I struggle, put me down carefully on the ground.

Feeding Time

I'm hungry! Purr-lease give me my dinner! I need food and water every day. You can feed me dry or wet food, which you can buy from a grocery store or pet shop. Read the label to find out how much food to give me.

Kitty's Top Meal-Time Tips

🐾 Grown-up cats like me need two meals a day. Kittens need three or four smaller meals.

🐾 Please give me clean water to drink. Cow's milk can make me sick.

🐾 Feed me in a quiet corner of the kitchen where I won't be disturbed.

🐾 Put my food and water bowls well away from my **litter tray**.

Coat and Claws

Cats are very clean creatures. I spend lots of time washing my fur. But you can help by **grooming** me gently with a soft brush. If your cat has long hair, you need to brush it every day to stop its fur from getting tangled.

scratching post

I need to keep my claws nice and sharp. Outside, I can scratch them against wood and tree trunks. Indoors, please give me a **scratching post** to use, covered in carpet or rope.

Play Time

All cats love to play. You can buy special cat toys, but ping-pong balls, boxes, and cardboard tubes also make good toys.

Make sure I have plenty of things to play
with, otherwise I'll get bored and unhappy.
I'll also need safe places for climbing
and perching.

Keeping Your Indoor Cat

All cats need a collar and **tag** with your name and phone number on it. Even if you have an indoor cat, it could escape and get lost. The tag helps people return your cat to the right home. You can also ask your vet to give your cat a **microchip**.

litter box

Many cats live indoors. This means they need to use a **litter box** to go to the bathroom. Keep the litter box in a quiet spot far away from its food bowls. Clean the litter box out every day. Wash your hands afterward.

Visiting the Vet

When I come to live with you, please take me to the vet for a checkup. After that, I'll need to go once a year for shots to stop me from catching bad diseases. Also take me to the vet if I seem sick or stop eating my food.

The vet will also treat your cat for **fleas** and **worms**.

There are lots of unwanted cats and kittens. When your cat is four months old, ask your vet about having it **neutered**. This means doing a small operation to stop it from having babies. It doesn't hurt, and your cat will quickly get better afterward.

Vacation Care

If you go on vacation you can't take me with you, so you need to find someone to look after me while you're away. Ask a friend or neighbor to visit your home every day to give me food and water.

Otherwise, you can bring me to a **kennel**. Kennels are places where people can bring their cats while they are away. Special pet handlers care for the pets and keep them company until their owners come back.

Cat Facts

 Pet cats are related to African wildcats.

 In ancient Egypt, cats were worshipped as gods. When a cat died, its body was made into a mummy.

 A cat's tongue is covered in tiny, sticky hooks. These work like the teeth on a comb when the cat licks and **grooms** its fur.

 In the wild, cats spend 6 to 8 hours a day hunting. Then they sleep for around 12 to 18 hours a day.

Helpful Tips

🐾 Cats rely on smell to tell them what is safe. A few days before you bring your cat home, take a blanket to the shelter. Your cat can get used to the smell and add its own smell. Then put the blanket in the cat's basket at home.

🐾 If you introduce a dog to a cat, keep the dog on its leash. Reward it for staying calm. Give your cat the chance to get away if it needs to.

🐾 Make sure the **scratching post** is tall enough for your cat to stretch out on and strong enough for it to lean on.

🐾 Never leave your cat alone with wool or string. Your cat may swallow it, or it may get wound around your cat's body.

Glossary

cat litter special gravel used to fill a litter box

fleas tiny insects that can live on a cat

grooming brushing or cleaning your cat's fur

kennel a place that looks after cats and dogs when their owners go on vacation

litter box a tray filled with cat litter where a cat can go to the bathroom

microchip a tiny chip that is put under a cat's skin. It has a number that can be read by a scanner if your cat gets lost.

neutered when a cat has an operation that means it cannot have kittens

scratching post a wooden post covered in rope or carpet. A cat scratches it to sharpen its claws.

tag a metal circle that attaches to a cat's collar

worms worms that grow inside your cat and can make it sick

Find Out More

Books

Mattern, Joanne. *All About Cats* series. Mankato, Minn.: Capstone, 2012.

Perkins, Wendy. *American Shorthair Cats.* Mankato, Minn.: Capstone, 2008.

Whitehead, Sarah. *How to Speak Cat!* New York: Scholastic, 2008.

Internet Sites

Facthound offers a safe, fun way to find Internet sites related to this book. All of the sites on Facthound have been researched by our staff.

Here's all you do: Visit www.facthound.com
Type in this code: 9781432971304

Index